fire *of* love

music for contemplative worship
Margaret Rizza

Kevin Mayhew

We hope you enjoy the music in this book. Further copies are available from your local music shop or Christian bookshop.

In case of difficulty, please contact the publisher direct by writing to:

The Sales Department
KEVIN MAYHEW LTD
Buxhall
Stowmarket
Suffolk
IP14 3DJ

Phone 01449 737978
Fax 01449 737834
E-mail info@kevinmayhew.com

Please ask for our complete catalogue of outstanding Church Music.

Fire of Love is available as follows:

1450114 **Vocal score** includes the melody, keyboard, guitar and optional vocal parts
1400195 **Melody edition** includes melody line, text and guitar chords
1480052 **Cassette** includes all fourteen pieces directed by Margaret Rizza
1490036 **CD** includes all fourteen pieces directed by Margaret Rizza

First published in Great Britain in 1998 by Kevin Mayhew Ltd.

© Copyright 1998 Kevin Mayhew Ltd.

ISBN 1 84003 278 2
ISMN M 57004 470 2
Catalogue No: 1400194

0 1 2 3 4 5 6 7 8 9

Front cover photograph reproduced by courtesy of SuperStock Ltd, London

Cover design by Jaquetta Sergeant

Music Editors: Nicola Caporali and Donald Thomson
Music setting by Geoffrey Moore

Printed and bound in Great Britain

Contents

Foreword

Give thanks to the Lord upon the harp,
with a ten-stringed lute sing him songs.
O sing him a song that is new,
play loudly, with all your skill.

Psalm 32 (33):2, 3

It is more than a year now since *Fountain of Life* came into being. I have been so moved by the wonderful response to this first collection from people all over the world. It has shown me that this Spirit of Love who prompted and inspired me to write these compositions has been very much alive and active, enkindling and uniting us all into this stream of prayer through music.

And so it was very much in a spirit of joy and thanksgiving that I embarked on this second collection: *Fire of Love.*

All the compositions are again in a simple contemplative vein and are a mixture of chants and choral pieces.

I found it to be a melting pot of struggles and searchings; of fleeting insights where one hovers between two realities; a mixture of darkness and light; of joy, of praise and of thanksgiving.

When I came to the poem of St John of the Cross, *Living Flame of Love,* to which I felt so drawn, I asked myself how I could possibly write music to such sublime words – it somehow seemed so presumptuous; even St John, when he writes to Doña Ana de Peñalosa, points out:

'I have felt, very noble and devout Lady, somewhat reluctant to explain these four stanzas as you asked. Since they deal with matters so interior and spiritual, for which words are usually lacking – in that the spiritual surpas ses sense, I find it difficult to say something of their content.'

To begin with I resisted the pull to put these very beautiful words to music, but in the end I found myself yielding to the gentle but insistent spirit of the poetry which drew me headlong into the soul's longing to be in union with its creator.

Most of the fourteen pieces can be sung and played according to the musical abilities and resources of the parish. They are infinitely expandable and can be used in many different ways.

I have many people to thank who have helped me during these months of writing the music: my beloved family who very often have to cope with a hermit-like wife and mother; St Thomas' Music Group and the Church with whom I have shared many things and who are such an important part of the music-making; my publisher who has always given me so much support and encouragement, and the many people involved with the publishing and recording of this music; and the Christian Meditation Communities (WCCM) who over the years have become an intrinsic part of my life.

And so again my hope is that this music will be a way of prayer; a way to still the mind so that our hearts may be open to the transforming work of this living, loving, life-giving eternal Spirit who strengthens and empowers us to build for his Kingdom on earth.

MARGARET RIZZA

About the composer

Margaret Rizza [Lensky] studied at the Royal College of Music, London, and the National School of Opera, London, and completed her operatic training in Siena and Rome. She has sung at many of the world's leading operatic venues, including La Scala, Milan, Glyndebourne, Sadler's Wells and with the English Opera Group, and under such conductors as Benjamin Britten, Igor Stravinsky and Leonard Bernstein. She was also a frequent broadcaster.

Since 1977 she has taught singing and voice production at the Guildhall School of Music and Drama, and gives master-classes and workshops at summer schools. She also devotes much of her time helping students to perform and share their music with the marginalised and with people with mental and physical disabilities. In recent years she has worked closely with music therapists.

She has trained and conducted several choirs, and is the founder of The Cameo Opera, The Cameo Singers and the St Thomas' Music Group.

Since 1983 she has dedicated herself to the work of spirituality and to the wider aspect of music in the community. She has led many retreats, and is closely involved with the Christian Meditation Centre, London. She is the Kent Co-ordinator for the South-East Region for Prayer Groups. She has also been involved in leading courses for prayer guides, parish Scripture courses and workshops for parish readers.

Her first collection, *Fountain of Life*, is also available from Kevin Mayhew.

Singing these chants

You will find that in using this music most of it can be done very simply indeed by the smallest of groups, singing in unison, or it can be expanded to incorporate much larger forces who have more diverse musical resources at their disposal.

I would like to give some suggestions for both these groups but, having said this, they are only guidelines and in the end it is you who will decide. Do be adventurous and work on variety. It is lovely to hear the different voices being highlighted, sometimes male, sometimes female, sometimes solo, sometimes children's voices; and then to hear the different colours of the vari ous instruments – all facets of God's life, love and beauty being revealed, poured out and manifested through our musical gifts.

There will naturally be more freedom of choice in the chants which can be as short as 2-3 minutes or as long as 8-10, minutes but even in the other compositions much can be adapted to accommodate the various resources which you have available.

The following chant patterns are the ones used for the recording of *Fire of Love*, but as I have pointed out there are many different ways of working the chants, and in the end it will be your choice.

'A BLESSING' CHANT PATTERN

1. Introduction: organ.
2. Chant melody: oboe.
3. Sopranos.
4. SATB voices with cello.
5. Instrumental interlude: violin with SATB voices on 'ah'.
6. SATB with oboe and cello.
7. SATB singing 'ah' with soprano descant.
8. Unison voices singing final bars.

'CALM ME, LORD' CHANT PATTERN

1. Introduction: violin.
2. Men, unison with cello *basso continuo*.
3. Unison voices.
4. Unison voices with oboe
5. SATB.
6. SATB singing accompanying harmony with cello.
7. SATB singing accompanying harmony with violin variation and cello playing the theme.
8. SATB singing accompanying harmony with recorder.
9. SATB.
10. SATB with soprano descant.

CHRISTUS NATUS EST

Two versions – for unison singing or SATB – are given.

'ENFOLD ME IN YOUR LOVE' CHANT PATTERN

1. Introduction: oboe.
2. Verse 1: soprano solo or choir in unison.
3. Introduction to verse 2: flute duet.
4. Verse 2: sopranos and altos.
5. Verse 3: SATB with oboe.
6. Instrumental interlude: violin and cello.
7. Verse 4: baritone solo or choir in unison.
8. Introduction to verse 5: recorder.
9. Verse 5: tenors and baritones.
10. Verse 6: SATB with oboe; continue into last-time bars.

Alternatively, this may be performed as a hymn by unison or SATB voices.

'EXAUDE NOS, DOMINE' CHANT PATTERN

1. Unison voices.
2. SATB voices.
3. SATB with violin.
4. SATB with soprano descant.
5. SATB singing 'ah' with cello.
6. SATB singing 'ah' with oboe.
7. SATB singing 'ah' with oboe duet.
8. SATB voices singing final bars.

FIRE OF LOVE

This is intended to be sung straight through as indicated in the score.

'IN THE LORD IS MY JOY' CHANT PATTERN

1. SATB humming.
2. SATB humming with soprano melody.
3. SATB on words with soprano melody.
4. SATB on words with violin.
5. SATB with cello duet.
6. SATB with soprano descant.
7. SATB singing 'ah' with oboe duet.
8. SATB singing 'ah' with flutes or recorder.
9. SATB singing words with soprano descant singing 'ah'.
10. SATB humming with soprano melody.
11. SATB singing words.

JESUS IS OUR JOY

Two versions – for unison singing or SATB – are given.

PRAYER OF ST PATRICK

Two versions – for unison singing or SATB – are given.

'SANCTUM NOMEN' CHANT PATTERN

1. Introduction: oboe
2. Choir unison: repeat the first six bars. Oboe joins on the repeat.
3. Choir SATB.
4. Choir SATB with violin.
5. Choir SATB with cello.
6. Choir SATB with soprano descant and flute, into last-time bars.

'TAKE MY LIFE, LORD' CHANT PATTERN

1. Introduction: oboe.
2. Verse 1: child solo, repeated by unison voices.
3. Violin.
4. Verse 2: men sing four bars then women sing four bars; all eight bars are then repeated by SATB voices.
5. Cello.
6. Verse 3: men sing four bars then women sing four bars; all eight bars are then repeated by SATB voices with oboe.
7. SATB humming with flute; continue into final bars.

THE GRAIL PRAYER

This is intended to be sung straight through as indicated in the score.

THE LORD IS MY LIGHT

Two versions – for unison singing or SATB – are given.

'THOU ART ALL THINGS' CHANT PATTERN

1. Introduction: flute.
2. Refrain 1: sopranos.
3. Verse 1: baritone solo sings four bars then soprano solo sings four bars with cello.
4. Refrain 2: unison voices with oboe.
5. Verse 2: men sing four bars then women sing four bars.
6. Refrain 3: SATB with violin.
7. Verse 3: SATB
8. Refrain 4: SATB with oboe duet.
9. Refrain 5: SATB with flute.
10. Last time bars: sopranos sing words; ATB humming.

The instrumental parts given within this score are intended to be interchangeable to enable you to make the best use of the available resources. Parts for C instruments may be played by either flute, oboe, violin or recorder; parts for B♭ instruments by clarinet, soprano/tenor saxophone or trumpet; parts for E♭ instruments by E♭ horn or alto/baritone saxophone and parts for bass clef instruments by cello, bassoon or double bass.

SANCTUM NOMEN

My soul magnifies the holy name of the Lord

Text: Traditional
Music: Margaret Rizza

MIXED VOICES

Sanc - tum no - men Do - mi - ni mag - ni - fi - cat a - ni - ma me - a.

Sanc - tum no - men Do - mi - ni mag - ni - fi - cat a - ni - ma

Last time *dim. e rall. al fine*

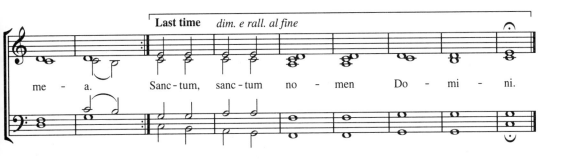

me - a. Sanc - tum, sanc - tum no - men Do - mi - ni.

VOCAL VARIATION

Soprano Descant: Final Chant

Ah,

ah,

To last time bars

ah.

11

INSTRUMENTAL PARTS

C INSTRUMENTS

Tranquil (♩ = c.63)
Introduction
Oboe

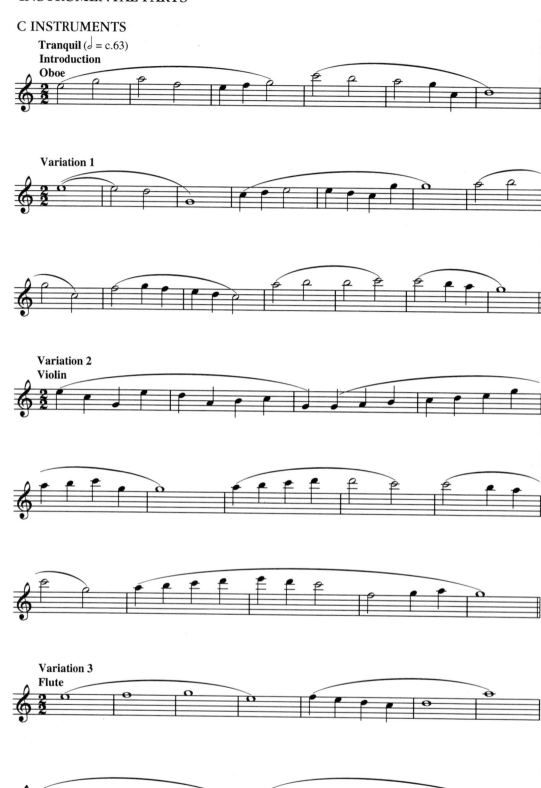

Variation 1

Variation 2
Violin

Variation 3
Flute

Tranquil ($\stackrel{\downarrow}{} = $ c.63)

Introduction

Variation

Cello I

Cello II

Last time

rall. al fine

rall. al fine

ENFOLD ME IN YOUR LOVE

You are the light that is ever bright

Text and Music: Margaret Rizza

2. You are the beauty that fills my soul,
   you by your wound make me whole,
   you paid the price to redeem me from death;
   yours is the love that sustains every breath.
   O hold me, enfold me in your love.

Optional harmony

3. You still the storms and the fear of night,
   you turn despair to delight,
   you feel the anguish and share in my tears,
   you give me hope from the depth of my fears.
   O hold me, enfold me in your love.

Instrumental Interlude
Unison

4. You are the word, full of life and truth,
   you guide my feet since my youth,
   you are my refuge, my firm cornerstone;
   you I will worship and honour alone.
   O hold me, enfold me in your love.

5. You have restored me and pardoned sin,
   you give me strength from within,
   you called me forth and my life you made new.
   Love is the binding that holds me to you.
   O hold me, enfold me in your love.

Optional harmony

6. You are the way, you are truth and life,
   you keep me safe in the strife.
   You give me love I cannot comprehend,
   you guide the way to a life without end.
   O hold me, enfold me in your love.

see overleaf for mixed voices

3. You still the storms and the fear of night, you turn de-spair to de - light,
6. You are the way, you are truth and life, you keep me safe in the strife.

you feel the an - guish and share in my tears, you give me hope from the
You give me love I can - not com-pre-hend, you guide the way to a

To verse 4   D.C.

depth of my fears.
life with-out end.   O hold me, en-fold me in your love.

Last time   *rall.*   *ten.*

hold me, en-fold me in your love, O hold me, en-fold me e - ver - more.

ten.

INSTRUMENTAL PARTS

C INSTRUMENTS

See overleaf for Oboe variation with verse 6 and bass clef part.

Variation with verse 6

BASS CLEF INSTRUMENT

($\bullet$ = 84)

Introduction and Interlude   **𝄋 Verse**

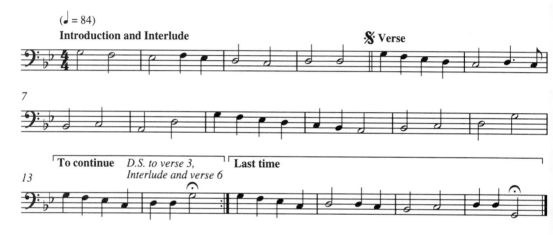

THE GRAIL PRAYER

Text: Traditional Prayer
Music: Margaret Rizza

way; I give you my eyes to see as you do; I give you my tongue to speak your words; I give you my mind, Lord, that you may think in me; I give you my spi - rit that you may pray in me, that you may pray in me.

Flute

mp

Glockenspiel

p

Choir in unison

Lord

Je - sus, I give you my hands to do your work; I give you my feet to go your

way; I give you my eyes to see as you do; I give you my tongue to speak your

words; I give you my mind, Lord, that you may think in me; I give you my

self that you may grow in me, so that it is you, Lord Je - sus, who

(ah,)

live and work and pray in me; I give you my whole self, that you may

that you may pray in me; I give you my

(Hum)

heart, Lord, that you may love in me,

INSTRUMENTAL PARTS

C INSTRUMENTS

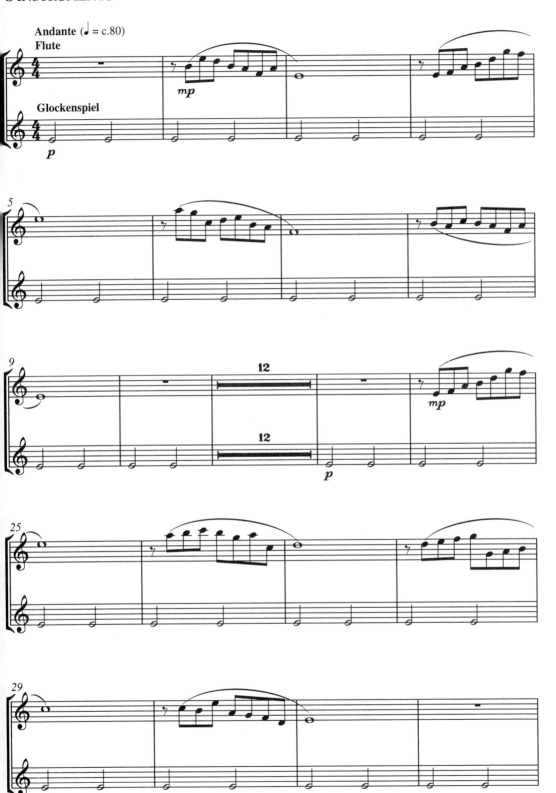

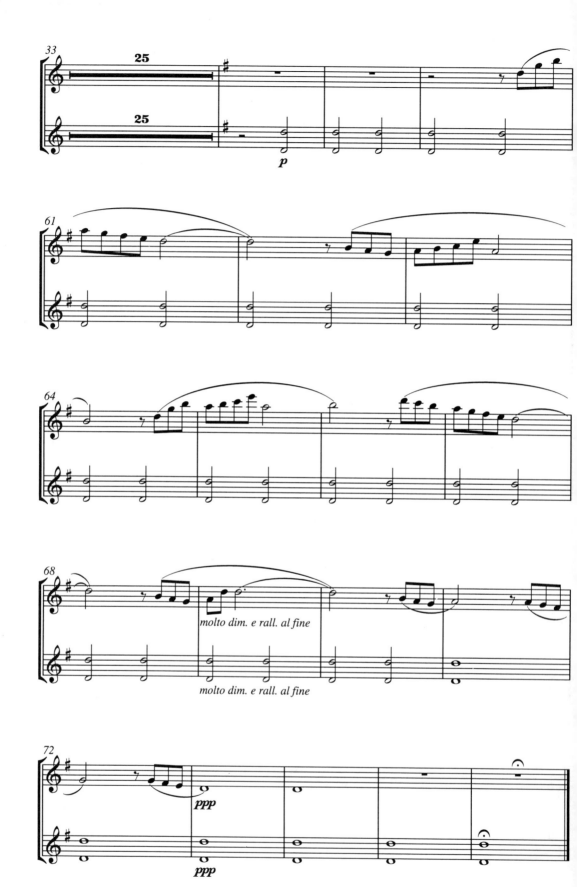

* Bars in brackets are optional.

IN THE LORD IS MY JOY

Text and Music: Margaret Rizza

MIXED VOICES

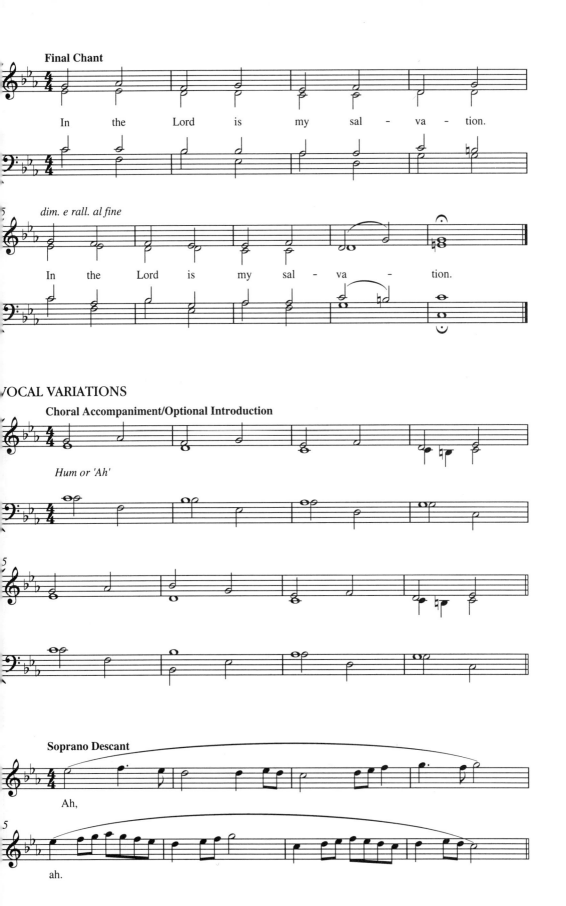

Final Chant

In the Lord is my sal - va - tion.

dim. e rall. al fine

In the Lord is my sal - va - tion.

VOCAL VARIATIONS

Choral Accompaniment/Optional Introduction

Hum or 'Ah'

Soprano Descant

Ah,

ah.

INSTRUMENTAL PARTS

C INSTRUMENTS

Bb INSTRUMENTS

Andante (♩ = c.76)
Variation 1

Variation 2

Eb INSTRUMENTS

Andante (♩ = c.76)
Variation 1

Variation 2

BASS CLEF INSTRUMENTS

Variation 3

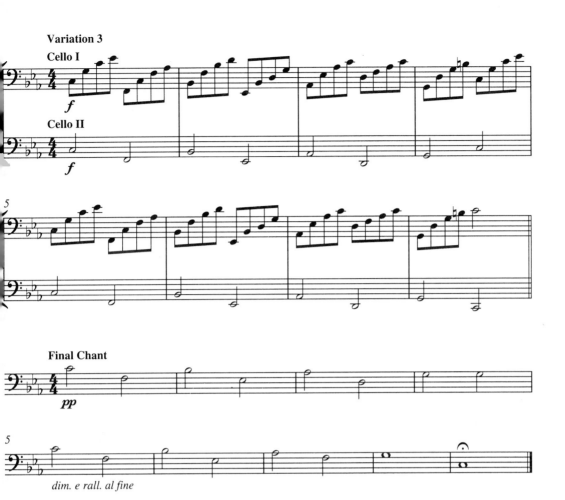

Final Chant

dim. e rall. al fine

35

CHRISTUS NATUS EST

Alleluia, glory to God on high.
Christ is born of the Virgin Mary.

* SIMPLE VERSION

Text: Traditional
Music: Margaret Rizza

* *See page 40 for Choral Version.*

VOCAL VARIATIONS

fire
of love

CHRISTUS NATUS EST

Alleluia, glory to God on high.
Christ is born of the Virgin Mary.

* CHORAL VERSION

Text: Traditional
Music: Margaret Rizza

* *See page 36 for Simple Version.*

ex Ma - ri - a Vir - gi - ne, al - le - lu - ia!

Chris - tus na - tus est, Chris - tus na - tus est,

ex Ma - ri - a Vir - gi - ne, al - le - lu - ia!

Chris - tus na - tus est, Chris - tus na - tus est,

Semi-chorus (or C Instruments)

Ah,

Full Choir (unison)

Chris - tus na - tus est, Chris - tus na - tus est,

(ah.)

ex Ma - ri - a Vir - gi - ne, glo - ri - a in ex - cel - sis De - o.

ex Ma - ri - a Vir - gi - ne, al - le - lu - ia!

f sostenuto

glo — ri - a, glo — ri - ia, glo — — ri - a.

ex Ma - ri - a Vir - gi - ne, glo - ri - a in ex-cel - sis De - o.

cresc.

1. Flutes and Oboe I
2. Violins and Oboe II

rall.

f cresc.

f cresc.

Al - le - lu - ia, glo - ri - a, al - le - lu - ia, glo - ri - a, glo - ri - a, glo - ri - a,

f cresc.

Al - le - lu - ia, glo - ri - a, al - le - lu - ia, glo - ri - a, glo - ri - a, glo - ri - a,

f cresc.

f cresc.

rall.

INSTRUMENTS

BASS CLEF INSTRUMENTS

cresc. poco a poco

cresc.   *f*

f cresc.   *ff*

rall. al fine

p   dim.   *ppp*

A BLESSING

Text: Gaelic Blessing, adapted by Margaret Rizza
Music: Margaret Rizza

May the Lord bless you, may the Lord pro-tect you and guide you, may his strength up-hold you, his light shine up-on you, his peace sur-round you, his love en-fold you.

VOCAL VARIATIONS

Choral Accompaniment

'Ah' or Hum

Soprano Descant (with Choral accompaniment)

Ah, ah, ah,

INSTRUMENTAL PARTS

C INSTRUMENTS

See overleaf for E♭ variation and bass clef part.

BASS CLEF INSTRUMENTS

($\quad$ = c.63)

Basso continuo and Final Chant

Last time

Variation

fire
of love

EXAUDI NOS, DOMINE

Hear us, O Lord; give us your peace

Margaret Rizza

Choral Accompaniment for Instrumental Variations

Do - na no - bis pa - cem.

Do - na no - bis pa - cem.

Final Chant

dim. molto al fine

Do - na no - bis pa - cem. Do - na no - bis

dim. molto al fine

lunga

pa - cem. Do - na no - bis pa - cem.

Finish with Hum

Soprano Descant

Ex - au - di nos, Do - mi - ne; do -

- na no - bis pa - cem tu - am.

INSTRUMENTAL PARTS

C INSTRUMENTS

Slow ($\beamed = c.58$)
Theme: Flute or Violin

Bb INSTRUMENTS

BASS CLEF INSTRUMENTS

THE LORD IS MY LIGHT

Text: from Psalm 27
Music: Margaret Rizza

* SIMPLE VERSION

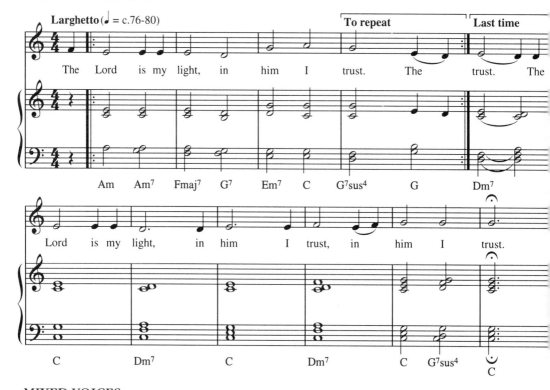

MIXED VOICES

* See page 64 for Choral Version

OCAL VARIATIONS

Unison Variation

The Lord is my light, my hope, my sal - va - tion; in
him I trust, in him I trust. The

Choral Variation

The Lord is my light, my hope, my sal - va - tion; in
him I trust, in him I trust. The

THE LORD IS MY LIGHT

Text: from Psalm 27
Music: Margaret Rizza

* CHORAL VERSION

* See page 62 for Simple Version

one thing I ask of the Lord: for this I long, to live in his house all the days of my life; to

Am   Am⁷   Dm⁷   G⁷   Em⁷   C   G⁷sus⁴   G

sa-vour the sweet-ness, the sweet-ness of the Lord; to be - hold his tem-ple; for this I long. The

Am   Am⁷   Dm⁷   G⁷   Em⁷   C   G⁷sus⁴   G

Lord is my light, my hope, my sal-va - tion; in him I trust, in him I trust. The

Am   Am⁷   Dm⁷   G⁷   Em⁷   C   G⁷sus⁴   G

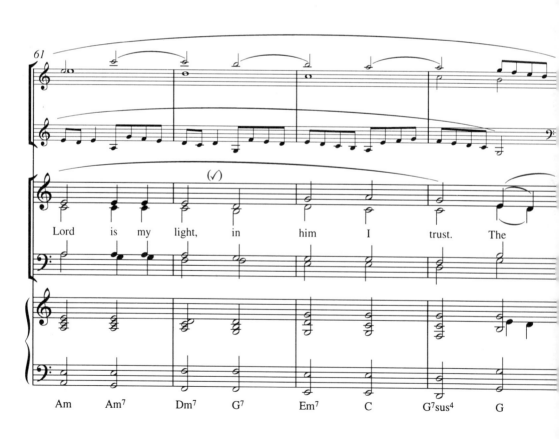

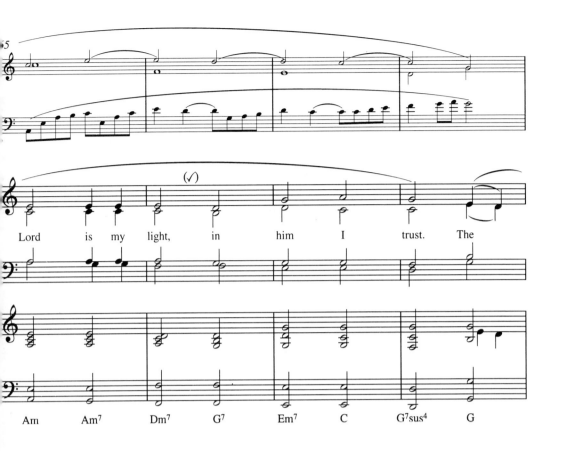

Lord is my light, in him I trust. The

Am   Am⁷   Dm⁷   G⁷   Em⁷   C   G⁷sus⁴   G

Soprano Descant

Ah,

Lord is my light, my hope, my sal-va - tion; in him I trust, in him I trust. There is

Am   Am⁷   Dm⁷   G⁷   Em⁷   C   G⁷sus⁴   G

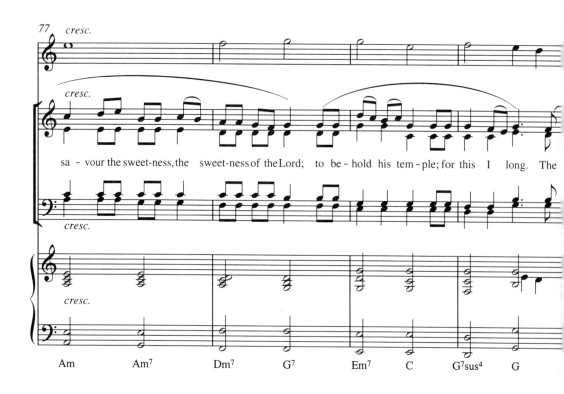

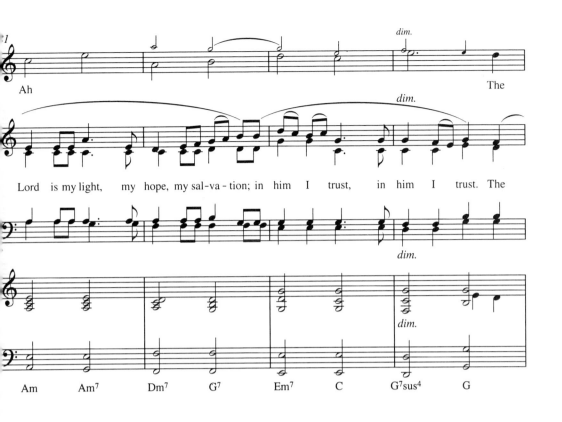

Ah ... The
Lord is my light, my hope, my sal-va-tion; in him I trust, in him I trust. The

Am   Am⁷   Dm⁷   G⁷   Em⁷   C   G⁷sus⁴   G

Lord is my light, my hope, my sal-va-tion; in him I trust, in him I trust.
Lord is my light, in him I trust. The

Am   Am⁷   Fmaj⁷   G⁷   Em⁷   C   G⁷sus⁴   G

Bb INSTRUMENT

BASS CLEF INSTRUMENTS

fire
of love

TAKE MY LIFE, LORD

Text and Music: Margaret Rizza

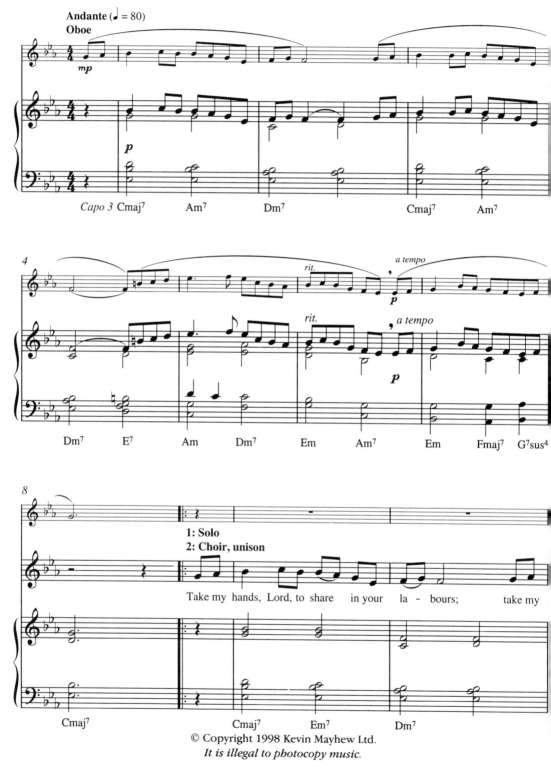

Take my hands, Lord, to share in your la - bours; take my

77

Cmaj7 Am7 Dm7 Cmaj7 Am7 Dm7 E7

rit. *a tempo*

rit. *a tempo*

p

p

Am Dm7 Em Am7 Em Fmaj7 G7sus4 Cmaj7

Oboe or Flute

1: Men, unison, on melody
2: SATB and Oboe or Flute

Keep my heart e-ver op - en to o - thers; may my time, Lord, be spent with those in

Cmaj7 Am7 Dm7 Cmaj7 Am7

1: Women, unison, on melody
2: SATB

need;   may   I   tend   to those who   need   your care.   Take my

Dm⁷   E⁷   Am   Dm⁷   Em   Am⁷

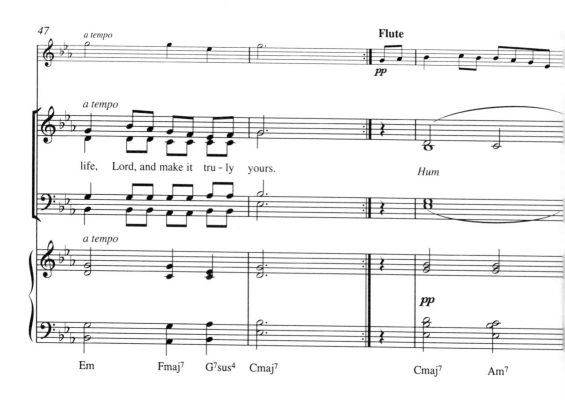

life,   Lord, and make it tru - ly   yours.

Hum

Em   Fmaj⁷ G⁷sus⁴ Cmaj⁷   Cmaj⁷   Am⁷

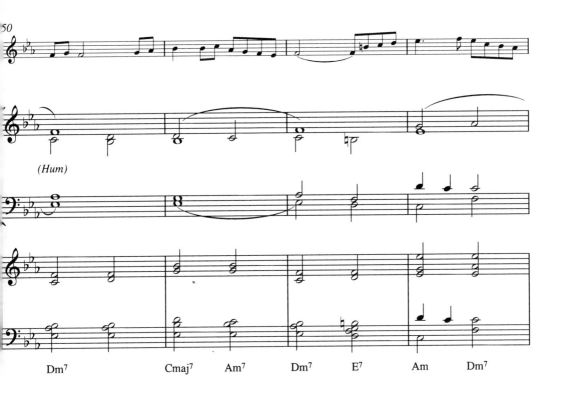

(Hum)

Dm⁷ .... Cmaj⁷ .. Am⁷ ..... Dm⁷ .... E⁷ ...... Am .... Dm⁷

(Hum) .... Take my life, ... Lord, and .. make .. it .. tru - ly .... yours.

Em ...... Am⁷ ...... Em ...... Fmaj⁷ .... G⁷sus⁴ .. G C

INSTRUMENTAL PARTS

C INSTRUMENTS

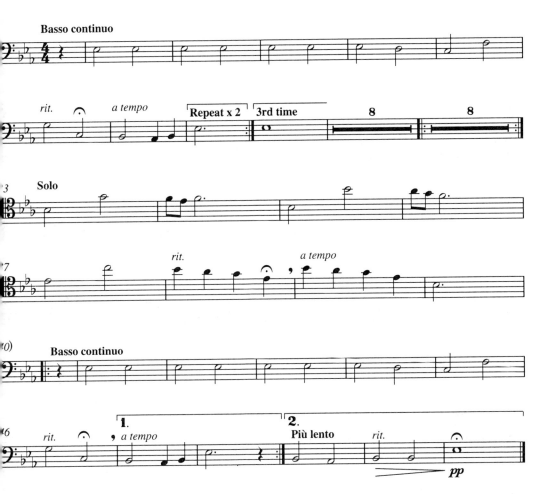

THOU ART ALL THINGS

Text: David Adam
Music: Margaret Rizza

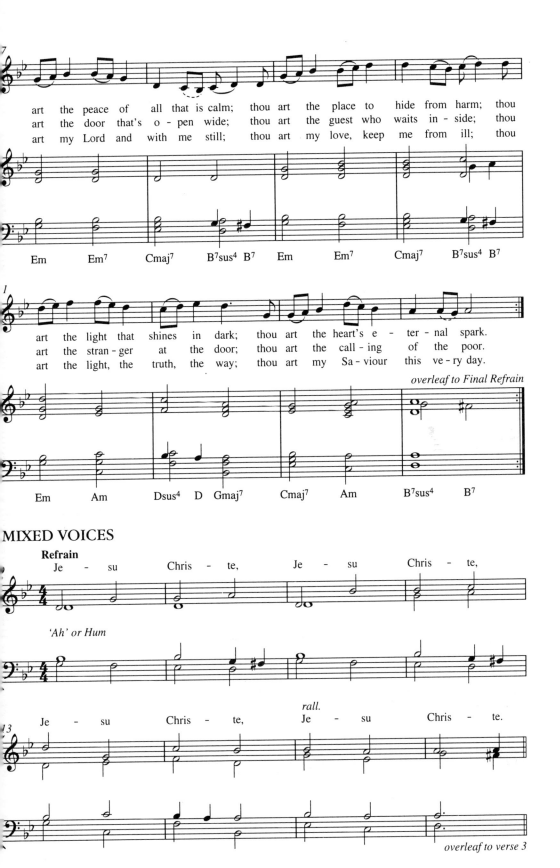

art the peace of all that is calm; thou art the place to hide from harm; thou
art the door that's o - pen wide; thou art the guest who waits in - side; thou
art my Lord and with me still; thou art my love, keep me from ill; thou

Em   Em⁷   Cmaj⁷   B⁷sus⁴ B⁷   Em   Em⁷   Cmaj⁷   B⁷sus⁴ B⁷

art the light that shines in dark; thou art the heart's e - ter - nal spark.
art the stran - ger at the door; thou art the call - ing of the poor.
art the light, the truth, the way; thou art my Sa - viour this ve - ry day.

overleaf to Final Refrain

Em   Am   Dsus⁴ D Gmaj⁷   Cmaj⁷   Am   B⁷sus⁴   B⁷

MIXED VOICES

Refrain

Je - su   Chris - te,   Je - su   Chris - te,

'Ah' or Hum

rall.

Je - su   Chris - te,   Je - su   Chris - te.

overleaf to verse 3

85

(16) **Last Verse**

3. Thou art my Lord and with me still; thou art my love, keep me from ill; thou art the light, the truth, the way; thou art my Sa - viour this ve - ry day.

Last time

Je - su Chris - te, Je - su Chris - te,

Em   Em⁷   Cmaj⁷   B⁷sus⁴ B⁷   Em   Em⁷   Cmaj⁷   B⁷sus⁴ B⁷

Je - su Chris - te, Je - su Chris - te.

Em   Am   D⁷sus⁴ D⁷ Gmaj⁷   Cmaj⁷   Am   B⁷sus⁴   B⁷   E

INSTRUMENTAL PARTS

C INSTRUMENTS

See overleaf for Flute Final Refrain and B♭, E♭ Instruments

87

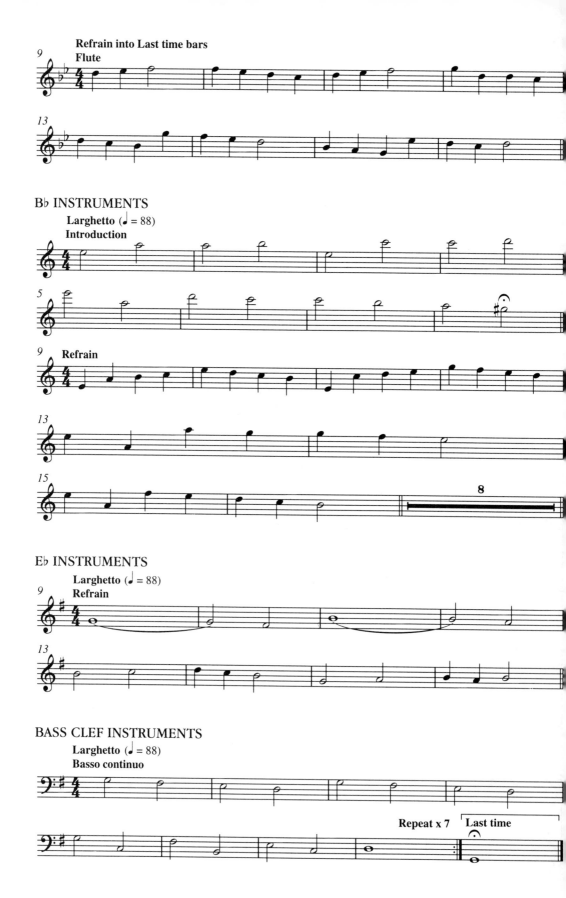

FIRE OF LOVE

Text: adapted from St John of the Cross by Margaret Rizza
Music: Margaret Rizza

will, per-fect in me this work of love; break through the veil of this sweet en - coun-ter.

O gen-tle dart, O ten-der wound, O soft hand, O lov - ing, car - ing

touch, that tastes of life e-ter - nal, life e-ter - nal, all debts are paid;

slay - ing, you changed death in - to life, slay-ing, you changed death in-to this fire of love.

Soprano Solo and/or Semi-chorus

O how gen-tle, O how lov-ing is your a-wake-ning deep with-in my

O how gen-tle, O how lov-ing is your a-wake-ning deep with-in my

heart. There se-cret-ly you dwell, hid-den and a-lone, breath-ing the sweet-ness of you

heart. There se-cret-ly you dwell, hid-den and a-lone, breath-ing the sweet-ness of you

love, en-kin-dled in your liv-ing flame, O how ten-der-ly you rouse me to love you.

love, en-kin-dled in your liv-ing flame, O how ten-der-ly you rouse me to love you.

p *veiled, mysteriously*

pp *veiled, mysteriously*

pp

Fire of love, fire of love, fire of love, fire of love,

pp

fire of love, fire of love, fire of love, fire of love,

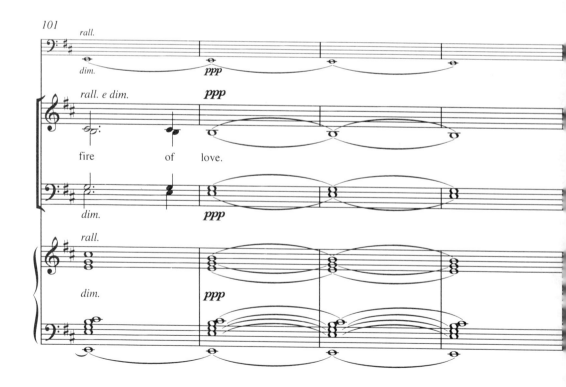

fire of love.

NSTRUMENTAL PARTS

INSTRUMENTS

CALM ME, LORD

Text: David Adam
Music: Margaret Rizza

Calm me, Lord, as you calmed the storm; still me, Lord, keep me from harm. Let all the tu-mult with-in me cease; en-fold me,

To repeat ad lib.

Lord, in your peace.

Last time

Lord, en-fold me in your peace.

VOCAL VARIATIONS

Accompaniment to Instrumental Variations

'Ah' or Hum

Soprano Descant for Final Chant

Ah.

103

INSTRUMENTAL PARTS

C INSTRUMENTS

Tranquillo (♩ = 108)
Theme: Violin

Variation 1
Oboe

Variation 2
Violin

Variation 3
Recorder

B♭ INSTRUMENTS

Tranquillo (♩ = 108)
Theme

PRAYER OF ST PATRICK

Jesus, Lord

Text: after St Patrick
Music: Margaret Rizza

* SIMPLE VERSION

* See page 108 for Choral Version.

Christ with me where-'er I go; Christ a - round, a - bove, be - low.
Christ con - trol my way-ward heart; Christ a - bide, and ne'er de - part.
Christ be my un - chang-ing friend, guide and shep - herd to the end.

Am⁷   Em⁷

Last time

Am⁷   Em⁷   Am⁷   Em⁷

morendo

Je - su Do-mi-ne, Je - su Do - mi-ne,

mp

morendo

Am⁷   Em⁷   Am⁷   Em⁷

rall. e dim al fine

Je - su Do - mi-ne, Je - su Do - mi - ne.

rall. al fine

dim.

Am⁷   Em⁷   Am⁷   Em⁷

PRAYER OF ST PATRICK

Jesus, Lord

Text: after St Patrick
Music: Margaret Rizza

* CHORAL VERSION

† *These 4 bars are repeated throughout the chant, ending on F♯ semibreve in the last bar.*
* *See page 106 for Simple Version.*

Sopranos and Altos

2. Christ be in my heart and mind; Christ with-in my soul en-shrined;

Am⁷   Em⁷

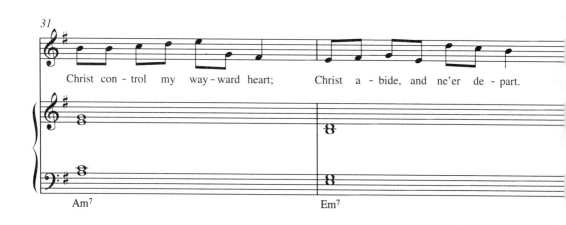

Christ con - trol my way - ward heart; Christ a - bide, and ne'er de - part.

Am⁷   Em⁷

Flute

Je - su Do - mi-ne, Je - su Do - mi-ne,

Am⁷   Em⁷   Am⁷   Em⁷

Christ be my un-chang-ing friend, guide and shep-herd to the end.

Am⁷   Em⁷

2 Flutes

mf

divisi

p

Je - su Do - mi-ne, Je - su Do - mi-ne.

p

mp

Am⁷   Em⁷   Am⁷   Em⁷

Soprano semi-chorus

mp

Je - su Do - mi - ne, Je - su Do - mi - ne.

p

Je - su Do - mi - ne, Je - su Do - mi - ne.

p

mp

Am⁷   Em⁷   Am⁷   Em⁷

112

7 **(Glockenspiel)**

(Soprano semi-chorus) *dim. e rall. al fine*

Je - su Do - mi - ne, Je - su Do - mi - ne.

Je - su Do - mi - ne, Je - su Do - mi - ne.

dim. e rall. al fine

ppp

Am⁷ Em⁷ Am⁷ Em⁷ Em⁷

INSTRUMENTAL PARTS

C INSTRUMENTS

BASS CLEF INSTRUMENTS

fire
of love

JESUS IS OUR JOY

Christmas Carol

Text: Pamela Hayes
Music: Margaret Rizza

* SIMPLE VERSION

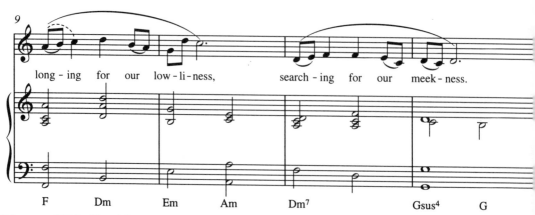

* See page 118 for Choral Version

2. Peace within our pow'rlessness,
   hope within our helplessness,
   hope within our helplessness,
   love within our loneliness.

3. Held in Mary's tenderness,
   tiny hands are raised to bless,
   tiny hands are raised to bless,
   touching us with God's caress.

4. Joy then in God's graciousness,
   peace comes with gentleness,
   peace comes with gentleness,
   filling hearts with gladness.

JESUS IS OUR JOY

Christmas Carol

Text: Pamela Hayes
Music: Margaret Rizza

* CHORAL VERSION

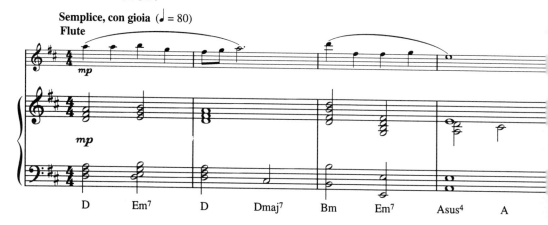

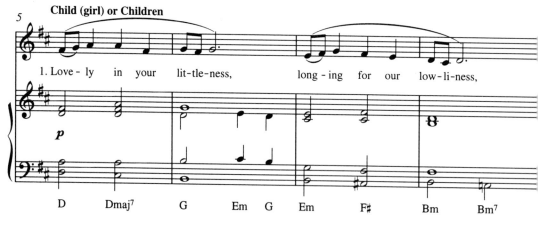

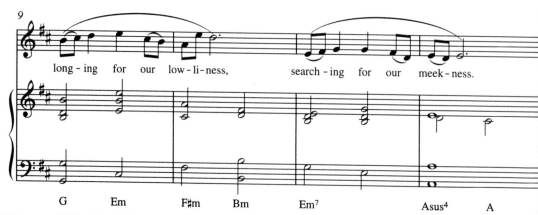

* See page 116 for Simple Version

Child (boy) or Children

2. Peace with-in our pow'r-less-ness, hope with-in our help-less-ness,

hope with-in our help-less-ness, love with-in our lone-li-ness.

2 Tenors and 2 Basses

Peace with-in our pow'r-less-ness, hope with-in our help-less-ness,

'Ah' or Hum

hope with- in our help-less-ness, love with- in our lone - li -ness.

('Ah' or Hum)

G   Em   F♯m   Bm   Em⁷   Asus⁴   A

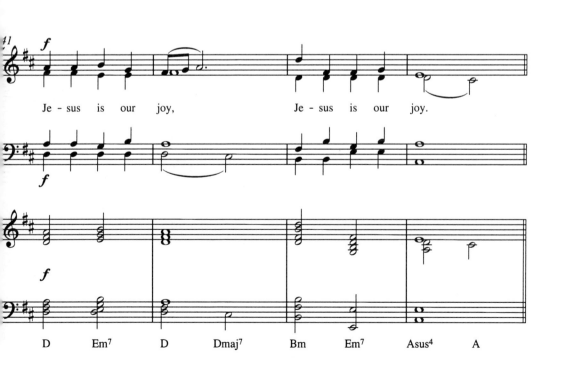

Je - sus is our joy, Je - sus is our joy.

D   Em⁷   D   Dmaj⁷   Bm   Em⁷   Asus⁴   A

3. Held in Ma-ry's ten-der-ness, ti - ny hands are raised to bless,

Hum

ti - ny hands are raised to bless, touch-ing us with God's ca-ress.

(Hum)

Violin and Recorder

Je - sus is our joy, Je - sus is our joy.

D — Em⁷ — D — Dmaj⁷ — Bm — Em⁷ — Asus⁴ — A

Soprano semi-chorus and/or Oboe

Ah,

4. Joy then in God's gra-cious-ness, peace comes with gen-tle-ness,

D — A — Bm — Bm⁷ — Em⁷ — Asus⁴ — A

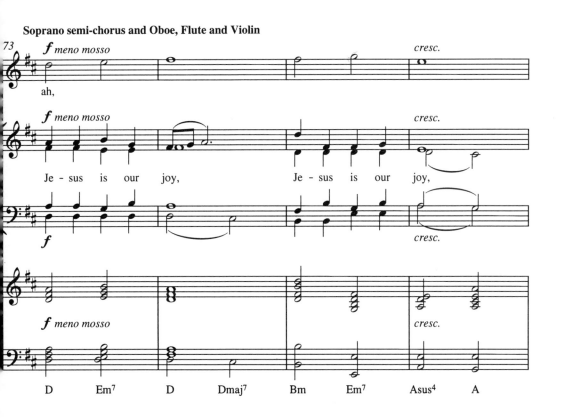

Soprano semi-chorus and Oboe, Flute and Violin

ah.

Je - sus is our joy, Je - sus is our joy.

F#m G A Bm Em⁷ A⁷sus⁴ A⁷ D

INSTRUMENTAL PARTS

INSTRUMENTS

BASS CLEF INSTRUMENTS